SAY BUMP
AND
TAKE A LEFT

MARY KATHRYN JOHNSON

ISBN: 098360181X
ISBN-13: 9780983601814

DEDICATION

To Duane, my incredible husband ~ Thank you for perfectly complimenting and supporting me in our many wonderful adventures, and here's to infinitely many more!

To Evan and Riley, my precious boys ~ Mommy Loves you, and counts herself as the luckiest person alive to be your mom! Here's to your many adventures and my cheering you through them.

CONTENTS

ACKNOWLEDGMENTS

I would not be anywhere near this point on my path were it not for the love and support of my wonderful in-laws (yes! in-laws) Bob and Jean Johnson. You both support and listen to me no matter how loud I get.
Thank You!
Andrea, Tina, Laurie, Clare and Shannon ~ You are all incredible women and moms (of babies and/or puppies), and your love, support and constructive criticism has helped me grow.
Thank You!

To all the moms and dads who sacrifice to stay home and raise their own children: When it gets tough, please remember that you are part of a small, yet wonderfully responsible, global family, and we thank you for helping make the world a better place - one child at a time.

THE BUMP
OH MY GOD, WHAT HAVE I DONE?!

Would you believe that I started a business because I fell and broke both my legs while I was 8 months pregnant with my second son? There it was, my 'aha' moment, and I didn't recognize it as such until about 2 years after it happened. There was a lot going on at the time, so I use ignorance as my excuse. Unfortunately, the really important moments in life take me totally by surprise, and I become a little slow on the uptake. At least I finally realized it, and I acted on it. That leaves a regret open for some other dream I might leave on the shelf.

A great deal of skill was required for me to break both my legs at the same time. I'd like to say this was the result of a tragic auto accident, a harrowing ski accident or simply wearing 5" heels, but I can't. A unique series of events which, if they happened individually would not have even caused me to stumble, combined at one precise moment with my size 11 feet to change my life.

One afternoon in early September, 2001, with the sweet smell of California Indian Summer heat, my three year old son and I were invited to my neighbor's house to swim.

No, not September 11th, September 5th! I was lying in bed with my cast clad feet propped up on a pillow on that world-changing day of 9/11!

On September 5th, two days after my 38th birthday, we left the swim date around 4 p.m. so I could get ready for an evening meeting for my new job. I stepped out my neighbor's front door, and my little, insignificant world tumbled into chaos - literally!

Now, I had been to my neighbor's house plenty of times in the five years since we had moved to the neighborhood, but I had always entered and left either through the backyard gate or the garage door. My neighbor had two young children at the time, a boy aged 4 and a girl aged 5, and my 3 year old Evan played with them quite often back and forth between our two houses. He never went swimming without me, however. Because the kids had dried off to play with a new toy in the front room, this visit was unique in that we left like actual guests - through the front door.

This was my first obstacle.

The step from the front door threshold to the cement slab porch of my neighbor's house is unusually high. Over 9" in fact, when the local building code requires a stair riser to be no more than 7".

No, I didn't sue!

It may not seem like much, but those two extra inches made a huge difference in my landing that first step! Have you ever taken a step down the stairs and expected the bottom to be closer than it actually was? My stomach skipped just like my foot skipped that step!

Second obstacle - the three young children had also scrambled out the door around me. Kids this age don't wait patiently in line to march single file out a door after a raucous day of swimming. No, they are over-excited and exhausted at the same time, and not at all patient enough to wait for some pregnant old lady.

Since watching where I put my feet was almost impossible with the enormous baby hotel that had grown in front of me the previous eight months, I guess you could say this represented my third obstacle

Fourth obstacle - I was wearing sandals with a hard, cork sole.

No, they didn't have a heel!

Pregnant, wearing a bathing suit AND heels?! I'm not that stupid, or that young! I threw away those shoes the next day!

So, when I stepped out of the door, all four of these things contributed to the fact that I was a somewhat comical, if dangerous, Weeble-like pregnant woman.

Too bad I fell down.

My first step landed on the outside of my right foot. The sole of that sandal did not give, and allow me to somewhat gracefully correct myself. My foot snapped sideways onto the outside. I started to fall, and caught myself with my left foot, but stepped on the outside of that foot, too, landing on my ankle. This time, I heard a "pop". I proceeded to fall - not so gracefully so as to avoid taking any of the kids with me - down the remaining three cement steps, landing on my well-padded backside. There was a full 3 seconds of shocked silence. I dimly registered hearing a baby cry somewhere in the neighborhood. Yes, all the spectators to this new "Mommy Tumbling" sport were staring at me with wide, shocked eyes. I expected someone to put up their arms and yell, "GOAL!", but thankfully no one did.

My neighbor anxiously asked me, "Which one is it?" as I clutched my legs as best I could around my nearly full-term bump. To which I shakily replied, "Both!" The outside of my right foot, between my pinkie toe and my heel began to swell, as did my left ankle. Not a good sign. I was making a conscious effort not to cry like that distant baby so my anxious three year old wouldn't either. I carefully scooted myself, butt first, back up the three steps, and onto a bench on the landing, where I was urgently reminded that the first thing I was going to do when I got home was head for the bathroom.

Never again will I wait until I get home.

As my neighbor ran in the house to get the phone, I held myself like most little girls do when they have to go, but don't want to stop what they are doing. Bouncing a little on the bench, I didn't care about decorum in front of the three unusually quiet children staring at me. I did attempt to retain some dignity when my neighbor returned with the phone, however, by quickly moving my hand up to my swollen belly. This awkward movement was apparently not as successful as I would have liked, because she immediately asked me if I wanted a pad, "just in case?" So much for my feeble attempt to remain dignified.

Taking deep, calming breaths, I called my husband, Duane, and tried to explain to him why he had to come home early from work. He took this news as he takes all shocking, potentially dangerous life-changing news - with disbelief!

I know my husband's reactions well, because during our 27 years of marriage I have given him cause to display them all. Nothing in our lives together has taken what could be considered a "normal" path, so he should not have been surprised. In fact, one of my favorite pieces of literature is **The Road Not Taken** by Robert Frost, because I consider my life's journey to always be on the path that "was grassy and wanted wear". Duane describes our marriage as, "What would have happened had Romeo and Juliet lived", but the youthful, forbidden love story has been lived and told so many times that I'll leave it out of this one. If we do represent the non-tragic Shakespeare, the mythical Mr. and Mrs. Montague missed an amazing adventure!

Seven years after we were married, we split up.

Not because of any seven year itch, (although the words "seven year" and "itch" together have quite bizarre connotations), but because we went to different Universities to finish our undergraduate education. He went off to UC Santa Barbara, and I ventured off to UC Berkeley. We saw each other about once every 6 weeks when he flew home for a weekend. Those weekends were intense since we passionately studied each other in addition to the books. I would cry my eyes out Sunday night after dropping him off at the airport, and then prepare for life without him for another six weeks. I was not your typical UC Berkeley student . . . if there is such a thing. I was about six years older than 99% of my fellow undergrad's, I didn't party on weekends, I wore a wedding ring and I shaved my legs and armpits regularly.

The first frantic phone call for help Duane received from me was when we were on summer break during college in 1986. I was privileged enough to get a ride to the ER from the local Volunteer Fire Department Ambulance for this incident. I had sustained a concussion, many bruises and possible facial disfigurement when I was thrown from a horse, and kicked in the face by another horse during my summer job as a wrangler on a ranch in the small Northern California coastal town where we lived. I am VERY lucky in that the only lasting effect from this particular incident is slight nerve damage on the right side of my face. I only feel it when I get my teeth cleaned, something I hate more than anything else in life. I would rather experience advanced labor pains for 10 hours than walk into a dentist's office. But, if I want to chew anything harder than pudding for the next 30 years, I clench my bicuspids, and step into the torture chamber with my iPod connected head held high.

Speaking of labor, my first pregnancy ended at 8 weeks gestation with another frantic trip to the ER and a misdiagnosed

Ectopic Pregnancy, but a miscarriage all the same. Again, my poor husband received an unexpected phone call from me, only this time I was already in the Emergency Room. My second pregnancy ended with another miscarriage at 12 weeks gestation almost a year to the day after my first. I found out I was pregnant with my first son, Evan, less than three months after this pregnancy ended. (Duane says he will never trust me again when I say 'We're safe!') Every other woman in my family has had her first pregnancy before the age of 18, so I was almost convinced that since I started almost 20 years later my genetics dictated that I was too late, and my eggs and uterus gave up a long time ago. Thank God I was wrong, and genetics didn't dictate having kids before I was 18, family dysfunction did. Fortunately, I could overcome generations of family dysfunction easier than genetics.

Frantic trips to the hospital during pregnancy had become a pattern, and my third pregnancy didn't disappoint. I went into early labor, and was hospitalized for a week on drugs to stop it.

At my 32 week OB appointment, my doctor told me that I was in active labor, and she immediately hospitalized me. All I was feeling were period-like cramps, and with all the horror stories I had heard I thought, "This can't be labor!" It was, apparently, and I was unbelievably blessed that those cramps were all I felt until a month later when I was 6cm, and the Doctor broke my water to get labor moving along again. When the real labor hit, I realized that those labor horror stories were really sugar coated fantasies designed to lure stupid naive' first timers like me into thinking that labor couldn't be that bad!

That phone call to both my boss and my husband while I was drugged up to stop the labor was interesting to say the least. My boss at the time took the news in stride - just give someone else my responsibilities. My husband, however, went home and shoveled bark for 10 hours a day for the next four days. He would of course visit me every morning and evening, but the way he handles stress is unique to me - distraction rather than food. I was extremely hurt at first that he wasn't tearfully wringing his hands at my bedside all day as I lay in a drugged stupor trying not to have a baby. After all, that is what I would be doing if our roles were reversed. (Yeah right, like he would survive morning sickness, let alone labor!) It took me five years of sulking to realize that he did not shovel bark all day because he didn't love me. Quite the contrary, his bark shoveling was caused by his love for me, concern for our unborn child and his inability to control the situation and ensure our safety. He had to take control of SOMETHING, and the 20 yards of bark he had delivered the day before I went into the hospital was going to be shoveled into submission even if it killed him.

The poor man should have been prepared for this fall when I was 8 months along with my second son given my track record during pregnancy. Now that I write this all down, I am either extremely stupid, extremely lucky, or I'm doing penance for my youthful Juliet impression. I bet my mother would agree with the latter.

Even though this fall down my neighbor's front steps was scary, I was not at all alarmed about the health of the baby. I felt no tenderness, bruising or cramping around my abdomen. Since I knew my body very well during all my previous pregnancies, I knew that the baby was okay, and previous experience taught me that I certainly did not need an ambulance for my rapidly swelling foot and ankle.

After I had finally convinced my husband that he did indeed need to come home to take me to the ER, because I was not prone to any kind of site-specific water retention that would cause only one ankle and one foot to swell to three times its usual size, I then had to call my boss and cancel my meeting. Oh My God! I had to call another boss!

This was actually much more difficult! As I said, this was a new job, and I had been employed only one month. This might be enough to instill fear for my job, but there is more. If you have been paying attention, you have deduced that this company hired me when I was already 7 months pregnant! The American's with Disabilities Act aside, I held out no hope of being hired by anyone while I was so obviously pregnant that I couldn't have hidden my huge bump with the most stealthily conceived camouflage maternity wear.

I was originally unemployed and pregnant, because in April 2001, I was laid off from my commission only Executive Recruiting job in High Tech. I was one of those Head Hunters finding jobs for techies during the last few months of the dot com explosion. I had also lost my previous management job early in the year 2000 to a merger between the second and third largest staffing firms in the U.S. at that time. All in all, the 21st century was beginning with the worst year emotionally in my adult life . . . until my second son was born of course! I thought my luck had finally changed when this innovative, barrier-breaking President of Blue Ribbon Personnel hired a 7 months pregnant woman to start the Executive Recruiting branch of her 20+ year old staffing firm. Not only did this amazing woman hire me, but she put me on salary, AND allowed me to work part-time occasionally from home! Going from unemployment, to commission only, to this was like winning the employment lottery, and I have remembered her treatment of me to create my own unique environment in my company!

How could I let her and the company down on my first meeting after only a month?!

Well, gravity let me down, so there you go.

Forget emotionally, 2001 was also becoming my worst year financially, because at the time, I was the main financial support for my family. Since my first son was born in 1998, Duane and I shared the joys of raising him. Duane was home Monday through Thursday, and I was home Friday, Saturday and Sunday. I have met very few couples who have taken the Mr. Mom path, and I wonder if Romeo would have? Being Italian, I doubt it - I know, I am one. We had used our savings during my two previous job changes, and now I was out of work again with a baby due very soon. Disability certainly didn't cover my mortgage (which was thankfully lower than the California average) but at least it covered the groceries. The only logical option: Husband works Full Time while I sit healing my bones and finishing my baby-baking. I kept thinking that there was some message I was missing with all the bad luck I was having with jobs, but I just couldn't figure out what it was - I guess I was a little slow . . . again.

This amazing new employer of mine didn't even consider firing me, thank God, she simply said I could come back as soon as I liked after I delivered the baby and my newly healed legs. My newborn son and I both attended the company Christmas party three months later. If you can believe it, I actually found clothing in my closet that not only fit, but coordinated beautifully with my black "walking boot!"

In hindsight, my boss' response to my phone call canceling that first meeting was my first taste of the sweet lemonade I had all around me in this sour situation, but at the time all I could feel was fear and depression.

The rest of that fateful evening of September 5th went by in a blur. I was clearly in shock, and still deluding myself into believing I had just sprained my left ankle and stepped on a rock with my right foot. I came crashing back to reality as if slapped in the face, however when the Emergency Room Doctor came into my room with my X-Rays and said in a bored voice, "Well, you did it good. You broke them both." I actually think my husband still thought I was overreacting until those words were spoken.

The Doctor proceeded to tell me that I had fractured the fifth metatarsal bone in my right foot and shattered, YES SHATTERED, the lower fibula as it goes into my left ankle joint. I had to be reminded of these details the next day (or actually later that same day since it was already midnight), because all I really heard were the phrases, "casts on both legs up to the knee," and "6 - 10 weeks," and "possible surgery."

That last one woke me up.

"What?" I yelled in surprise. "I'm sorry, Doctor, but I don't think you understand that this big bump is really a baby!"

He said something about surgery being possible when, "one is pregnant," to which I replied "Go #@%& yourself!", or something somewhat cleaner since my 3 year old was present. I asked him, "Why would I accept any risks to my unborn child by consenting to surgery without a life threatening, or at least permanently disabling situation?!" Dr. Boredom just shrugged his shoulders. My husband quickly agreed, when he saw the look on my face, that we would talk about it tomorrow with the Orthopedic Doctor.

A technician proceeded to fit me with temporary casts and we made an appointment to return for the real things later that morning, at our first of many return trips to the hospital during the next three months. Evan, was a real trooper! He never fussed once, and stayed awake even in the shocked silence of the 45 minute car ride home around 1 a.m. He will make his future wife very happy if he continues to be so intuitive to the women in his life. She better thank me!

My first question for the Orthopedic Doctor later that morning was, "How could this happen?! All I did was step out a front door!"

His response made total sense, but I had never heard of it having these consequences. Apparently, there is a hormone called Relaxin that is released toward the end of the third trimester of pregnancy that is designed to soften and loosen the pelvic ligaments and cervix to prepare for labor and delivery. This hormone is supposed to allow your pelvis to expand and stretch without breaking as the baby travels down the birth canal.

Unfortunately, this hormone circulates throughout a pregnant woman's entire system and softens ALL ligaments. As if to add injury to the insult of my clumsiness, when I took that step out my neighbor's front door, my ligaments were too drunk with this hormone to do their job, and the weakest bones broke without the support of the ligaments staying tight around them. Since I had already gained about 30 pounds during the previous 8 months, those drunk ligaments had even more weight to try and reign in.

Why did I give in to those Starbucks Coffee Ice Cream cravings?!

The Orthopedic doctor suggested that we x-ray my left ankle again after the baby was delivered to see if the bones were healing properly, and decide then if surgery would be needed. (Fortunately, surgery was not necessary.) I chose pink and blue for the colors of my casts since we were still on that "road less traveled" by not finding out the sex of the baby. At home later that morning after the permanent casts were fitted, I lay in bed still in shock. I kept staring at these stumps covered in neon, with these 10 sausages pretending to be toes sticking out of them, and thought blithely, "Well, at least I just got my toes done." I couldn't hold it in much longer. When I was sure that my husband and son were safely on their way to the park, I let go, and cried like I haven't cried since the first time I saw the movie **Beaches**. My feeling of depression was more overwhelming than I could possibly describe.

"I can't do this!" I kept crying in anguish.

I was angry with myself.

I felt sorry for myself.

I had literally stumbled into this horrible situation.

Isn't that always the way the journey begins?!

INCONTINENCE AND A WALKER

I have learned a few things about myself in the 40+ years I have

lived. I happily admit to being stubborn, impatient and fiercely

independent. All three of these characteristics were the result of

my innate personality and living with my controlling father for the

first 18 years of my life - another story that has been lived and

retold by countless others. Now, I was faced with the inability to move without assistance. Two of those three character flaws I just mentioned had to be abandoned. A myth told by Joseph Campbell that kept ringing in my ears goes something like, "Be careful when casting out your demons, lest you cast out the best part of yourself." So, my stubbornness I clung to.

I was actually very lucky in that I had a walking cast on my right leg which allowed me to stand flamingo-like on that leg. How appropriate that this was the leg with my pink cast. I would not put any of my considerable weight on my left ankle however - thinking about "surgery" while pregnant had me following the Doctor's orders like a Star Wars Clone.

How did I get around you ask? A wheel chair was the first option, until I pictured the walls of my house being demolished and said, "No Thanks, what else?" We lived in a 1600 square foot tract home with a standard hallway connecting the bedrooms and garage to the front rooms and kitchen. Our home had a typical 3 bedroom/2 bath floor plan fit into a neat little box shape with no room for grand hallways and entrances. We have since remodeled and removed the hallway to open the house entirely. A day late and a dollar short, as they say, but nice all the same.

Next I was offered crutches.

PLEASE, PEOPLE! Being off balance with this big bump in front of me was the cause of the accident in the first place! What, you want me to break my neck too?! Instead, I was given a walker. Yes, a walker. You know, the things you see little old ladies using when they go out on the town.

No I didn't put tennis balls on the bottom!

I was instructed not to "hop" when I used the walker. I was supposed to pick up the walker while balancing on my right foot, move it forward about a foot, place it on the ground, lift the heaviest part of my leaning body off the ground using the support of my hands on the sides of the walker, swing my right leg forward into the open end of the walker and gently place my right foot on the ground again to support my weight, all the while not allowing my left foot to touch the ground. The bottom half of my body had an additional 50 pounds attached to it with my already curvy figure, the weight of the baby hotel and the casts so in essence, I became a human pendulum. I could just see myself flat on my ass again with the first attempt. Forget moving the walker a foot, I started with about 3". Several times I hit the front of the walker with my swinging right foot, and hoped like hell my arms would hold until I came to a full and complete stop. Let's see how strong you are when you are doing the equivalent of a push up with 50 extra pounds on your body. Not hop?! Yeah, right! If you can believe it, I actually lost weight in my eighth month of pregnancy. There were two good reasons for this:

1. I couldn't readily reach food whenever the mood or craving struck, and asking my husband to do my grazing for me was just sad.

2. Every time I did move, it was like I was attending water aerobics class minus the flowered swim caps and the water. My breath, like my dignity escaped me in gasps.

Do I really need to tell you how often I had to pee at this stage of pregnancy? Add that to the fact that I now moved at turtle speed, and it was obvious that the first "hop" on the way to the bathroom was going to open the flood gates.

So much for keeping the casts clean and dry.

A phone call to the hospital, and I happily was introduced to a bedside commode.

My husband also became intimately acquainted with this device when he had to empty and clean it twice a day.

On more than one occasion, I got a disgusted look from Duane as he attempted to carry, without spilling on our newly cleaned carpets, a too full commode to the toilet to dump it after a particularly productive night. Think about it . . . you ladies who have had babies know what comes out after you deliver with an episiotomy. My husband absolutely deserves a medal since I was still using this wonderful commode until my newborn was three weeks old! At least I know he will take care of me in my old age. Actually, when I'm 80 years old, soaking my teeth and forgetting his name, he might just say, "Hey Babe, I did my time 40 years ago, you're on your own!"

Laughter is the best medicine they say, and everything I did while pregnant and wearing pink and blue casts was a joke waiting to happen. If I didn't laugh at myself, I would have given in to the tornado of emotions I was feeling, and let myself be sucked into the cyclone. Resisting this tornado was one of the best training methods for self employment (even though a category F10 would probably best describe a self employment tornado). The laughter could not, however, keep the tornado from constantly churning my emotions all around me like so much dust in the air that I couldn't see or breathe properly. Emotions like sadness, guilt, anger, depression, frustration and misery. The laughter couldn't blow the emotional dust away completely, but it was at least kept out of my eye.

I had never actually been depressed before. I know, surprising with all the accidents I just chronicled during my marriage thus far. And, I didn't even go into the stuff that happened when I was a kid - like the time my younger sister ran over me with my dad's three-wheel trike. God, now I know what Bella in Twilight feels like!

Apparently, one of the symptoms of depression is that you don't realize the impact your depression has on your life. For example, I love to read. I will always find time to read. A good mystery can engage my mind, and if I'm lucky my spirit. If the only time I had in my day to read was when I was sitting nursing my newborn, I would coo and read, coo and read. You would think that sitting immobile on the couch with my second born would be a perfect excuse to read voraciously.

I didn't read one paragraph of one book for at least three months.

Please understand, I'm talking about reading for pleasure. Okay, I read the pamphlets when the baby came about his growth and development, but that was motivated by fear, not pleasure. The cloud of emotions swirled around me too fiercely to allow simple pleasures like reading.

I finally accepted that I was depressed. I had never experienced this, so I didn't know what was happening, but actually, that was a good thing! After about a week of sitting on the couch with my feet propped up, watching mindless T.V. reruns and zoning out into my depression, my wonderful partner gave me an emotional kick in the ass by telling me he was going back to work.

"No!" I said. "Who is going to play with Evan? Who is going to make his lunch? Who is going to watch him while I . . . while I . . . "

I saw this bewildered, sad look on my wonderful husband's face as he walked away. I realized then that I wasn't "Mom" anymore. Hell, I wasn't "ME" or any of the other countless titles I held in what was considered 'my life'. I was feeling sorry for myself - rightly so in my opinion - but my family was suffering, and so was I. I saw in that instant that by giving in to my depression, I was actually being quite selfish. I mean think about it. I was not permanently disabled, I was not ravaged by disease, I was not a woman living in the Middle East! I had to mentally shake myself and say, "Get Over It Woman! If you can still move, you better start doing it, otherwise you are going to get stuck like this - physically AND emotionally!"

Here was my first life changing realization:

I have complete power over how I feel and act.

There would be many more to come as I hopped through this unique journey, and they all helped me gain the confidence to take a left turn from safety and choose the rocky, uncertain road toward my dreams.

So, I crawled on the floor - hey, I could use my knees - and rolled the baby hotel over so I could sit on my butt and play. The look on my son's face almost made me dive into the swirling cyclone, but I thought crying right then might make him realize that mom had really flown the coop! I felt better, I felt in control and I didn't feel depressed anymore (not until I had to pee again 5 minutes later). I still couldn't walk, and hadn't a clue how I was going to make lunch, let alone get through labor, delivery and caring for a newborn, but I had gotten used to baby hops with my walker, so I decided to take it one hop at a time. I now know the power and purpose of the saying, 'Fake it 'till you Make it', only I now say 'Keep walking like you know where you're going.'

One thing in particular that my husband did that day and once a week during this ordeal helped tremendously with my frame of mind. He took me out on our patio in those beautiful early fall California days and washed my hair. I could only stand on one leg long enough to give myself a sponge bath once a day - I was not able to do many things, and I was determined to be clean while doing them - but I could not stand long enough to wash and rinse my long hair. I certainly couldn't take a shower until both casts were removed, and picture me trying to get in a bathtub while keeping both legs out of the water.

I'd drown next.

So, until my first cast was removed seven weeks into this ordeal, the one thing I looked forward to most was my weekly hair washing. I learned to celebrate the little things in life.

If your man has never lovingly washed your hair for you, ladies, you are missing one of the truly sensual experiences in life. Too bad we couldn't take advantage of it. Picturing further intimacies with my husband while I had an 8 month pregnant bump, a pink cast on one leg and a blue cast on the other is enough to induce belly shaking, pee my pants, crying fits of laughter. Amendment to my previous depression rule: the best things for depression are laughter AND action!

Building with Lego's helps too.

THE BIRTH
WHAT'S THAT SMELL?

As soon as I adjusted to my life with two casts and a Bump, I got rid of the Bump and acquired a newborn. This wasn't as easy as falling out a front door, however.

My in-laws were supposed to stay with us to take care of our three year old when I went into labor. As if Karma had taken control of my life, I actually broke my legs on the same day that my Mother-in-Law had knee replacement surgery. I have a great relationship with my Mother-in-Law, and I love her dearly. No, Really! Jean and I are the only two females treading water in this testosterone pool. Our knowing looks at each other are born of years of experience with the Johnson Men. Even though we are 30 years apart in age, and are products of totally different child rearing practices, hers from the MidWest and mine from California, this one common life experience made us kindred spirits. Okay, I did bug her about her weight, and claim that carrying it around with her for the last 30 years is what caused her OsteoArthritis, but that's not going to come back on me, is it?

I actually keep my mouth shut a lot more now, lest I create for myself the habits I complain about in others.

Well, my amazing Mother-in-Law hobbled her way to my home just two weeks after her surgery to take care of Evan when I went into labor. They lived three hours away, and my labor was short with my first delivery - 4 hours - so I was a bit nervous being 36 weeks pregnant that I would be delivering this one solo.

They arrived, and we waited.

I started to get irrational.

Did I say "started"?

My in-laws arrived on a Monday, and planned on returning home the following Friday if I hadn't popped yet. I really started to panic on Thursday night before bed, because I was convinced that if they left, Duane would have a relaxing day playing with our 3 year old while I pushed hard and cursed all men whose names begin with the letter 'D'!

I woke up around 2 a.m. on Friday morning for my second commode visit since falling asleep. I stood up, took a hop to my little friend, did my business, took a hop back to the bed and laid down to snooze until my next visit. I closed my eyes then felt something wet. I sat up and got the full effect of the break in my bag of water. I poked my husband and said, "My water just broke".

"Huh? Are you sure?" he mumbled.

"No," I said sarcastically. "I always wet the bed right after I visit the commode."

I was so relieved - literally and figuratively! My in-laws had to stay now! My relief vanished, however, with the arrival of my first real contraction. My Doctor had to break my water to keep labor moving with my first delivery, so I wasn't familiar with these uncontrollable spurts of peeing sensation.

Now that I'm 47, I no longer need the onset of labor to cause that.

The memory of what came next flooded my mind like my amniotic fluid was flooding my sheets.

If you have never given birth, I would have expected you to put this book down after the first page.

You'll put it down now.

You have missed one of life's smelliest adventures if you have never in your life had a cast anywhere on your body. The least smelly time with my casts was in the beginning, and not just because I had that shiny new cast smell. I didn't know this, having never experienced the joys of breaking a bone, but the casts needed to be changed after just one week. This had less to do with olfactory stimulation, and more to do with muscular degeneration, however. My calves now resembled bamboo poles, and the casts needed to be refitted so I didn't do more damage. I didn't need loose casts to do my damage, I had various bodily fluids.

My casts had occasionally gotten damp during my daily sponge baths, but I hadn't really noticed any smell until the amniotic fluid hit them. Unfortunately, I had to sit on my bed peeing and waiting for my husband to wake my in-laws and get my stuff in the car. My supposed irrational insistence on a waterproof mattress pad didn't seem so irrational anymore.

Labor had started in earnest now, and I knew it was going quickly. When we got to the hospital, my husband had to leave me in the car to commander my ride - a wheel chair. The nurses started to laugh when they saw me being wheeled through the door.

Really, they laughed!

I was checked into a labor room, trying to breathe through contractions, and nurses kept coming into my room from all over the hospital to see for themselves if the rumors were true. There really was a woman in labor with both legs in casts. My Mom finally showed up and took on the job of keeping the Nursepaparazzi at bay so I could focus and not kill someone when they interrupted me during a contraction. I'm one of those women who delivers her babies using what's called "natural child birth," AKA painful sadomasochism, because my fear of huge needles in my spine far outweighs my fear of labor pain.

Labor progressed quickly, about four hours again, and I was ready to push. Actually, I was trying to keep myself from giving in to this overwhelming urge to push. The nurse had just declared that I was dilated to 9 cm, and would probably be ready to push in about an hour. She was obviously a new understudy in my labor production. The shift change had just happened. Within five minutes of her departure, I was shaking the entire bed with each contraction, trying to divert the pushing urge, and screaming for her return. She confirmed a "10", and then told me there was a waiting line for the delivery room. The nurse actually had to convince the Doctor that I was a "good pusher" to move me up the queue.

I was quickly moved to the delivery room, and prep'd for delivery. One nurse held up my blue cast, and my husband held up the pink one, because there was no way my plastered feet were going to fit into those stirrups!

The Doctor was not in the room yet. She was delivering another baby, and my nurse was coaching me to push a few times to get the baby into position. Nurse Understudy still hadn't learned her part however, because one push and the head was half way out.

"Stop pushing and hold it in until the Doctor gets here!" was the next thing I heard.

That's It, She's Fired!

I actually yelled, "What?! Are you kidding?! Hold It In?!"

That last bit was shrill enough to interfere with the beeps on the monitors. I wanted to kick that nurse upside her head! She was in the perfect position, and I would have done it if I didn't have a baby's head between my legs!

I started screaming through clenched teeth, yelling, "Where's the Doctor?!" as I shook the delivery table again trying to divert the pushing urge.

What seemed like hours actually turned out to be about a minute, and the Doctor was there, gloved and ready to catch. Two more pushes and Riley was delivered and put on my rapidly deflating bump.

He didn't cry.

He wasn't breathing.

I rubbed him, and talked to him. The nurse whisked him away and my husband instinctively followed.

I finally heard a faint cry.

Glorious Relief!

My son was born, with a little help to get his breathing started, at a healthy seven pounds, two ounces. I couldn't hold Riley for about an hour, because he had to stay under the heat-lamp to get his temperature up to normal. When the nurse finally wheeled his little portable oven over to my bed, I saw that my little guy actually had a ring of bruises around his forehead. I guess my Kegel exercises were good for something.

When asked later how the delivery was, Duane said, "It stunk." I guess the placenta got involved in this olfactory game too.

Unfortunately, I wasn't scheduled to have my casts changed again for about two weeks. My newborn was going to bond to a smelly mom, and then be confused in two weeks. Luckily, I started breastfeeding immediately when Riley was removed from the heat lamp, and the saying, "The way to a man's heart is through his stomach" was proven correct yet again. Too bad my own sense of smell hadn't diminished after delivery. I couldn't stand myself for the next two weeks. How could I hop through this journey with a stinky green cloud following my every move? Here was another test of my patience, because I had no choice. Here was yet another lesson learned that has served me very well in self employment:

Even though it's messy, sometimes ya gotta do what ya gotta do.

I did have the choice while in my recovery room to either have Riley in the room with me or have him taken to the nursery. There was no way anyone was going to take him out of my sight once he came out of my body! I worked too hard for this one. I mean really, how much sleep do you get in the hospital anyway? He slept right where he ate. When the nurse came at 2 a.m. to take him to the nursery for weighing and measuring, I faced the first of many parenting decisions for a second born. I had gotten out of bed and followed my first born to the nursery for this procedure, was I going to slight my second born? Admittedly, Riley would never know if I was there or not, but I would. In that split second, I imagined telling both boys their birth stories in about 5 years, and letting this first bit of favoritism slip. How could I tell my teary eyed Riley that I didn't follow him to the nursery just because of a little thing like casts and a walker? I couldn't have that!

I think all the blood had rushed from my brain to my broken legs.

Anyway, I swung my neon legs over the side of the bed, and reached for my walker. The nurse looked at me with shock, and incredulity. I get that a lot actually. Anyway, the nurse must have thought that my brain had suffered a similar injury as my legs, but didn't argue as I prepared to take my first hop. Of course, the nursery had to be down two corridors, up one floor and down another corridor. I thought I better visit the bathroom first.

This nurse was all business. She only waited for me at the elevator and the nursery door. I got a good workout that day competing in the first ever Birth with Broken Bones Biathlon - delivering a baby and competing in a long distance walker race. The nurse did give me a compliment, however when we finally reached my room again, and sweat was pouring down my face. She said that she would use me as an example to any woman who said that she was too tired to get up and use the bathroom after delivery. You don't know anyone like that do you?!

I must admit, however that during my hospital stay I put those wonderful bed protection pads to good use when I let a little more come out than the normal afterbirth bodily fluids for which they were designed. Hey, I was tired, and wasn't used to having to hop to the bathroom 3 times an hour. I was too embarrassed to ask for another bedside commode even though I missed it more

than I missed my husband.

WELL WISHERS OR PEOPLE VISITING THE ZOO?

Phone calls were made and friends and relatives started to visit.

Seeing the look of awe on big brother Evan's face when he was

introduced to his little brother made any discomfort melt away.

For the next few hours I was caught up in the after glow of this

precious thing called life. What we can actually create is truly

miraculous.

Initial hospital visits by well wishers are always welcome. Mom and Dad are usually shocked and awed by the surreal experience they just had, and usually welcome the opportunity to tell their birth story to whomever will listen. A few of my friends and family who had not yet witnessed for themselves my pink and blue beached whale show thought that they would get a 2 for 1 special by visiting the hospital when I delivered the baby. I also think they felt that the hospital was more neutral territory where they wouldn't get roped into a chore like cleaning the bathroom or doing the dishes.

The next day I got to take my little miracle home. Getting ready to leave the hospital, I realized that I couldn't walk and carry him at the same time. I needed both my hands for the walker. Here was another blow to my independence. This one I really didn't like, and it would impact me even more when I got home. Think about all the things you do one handed while carrying your newborn around the house. I guess my second born would get the same attention as my first born - sit and stare at this amazing thing I'm holding all the time. At least here is one piece of "Mom guilt" I also didn't have to carry around.

The first couple of days being home with a newborn are always a challenge. The entire family is adjusting to its newest member, and the baby is, among many things, adjusting to breathing air instead of fluid. That black, tar-like poop isn't so cute and interesting the second time around. Most people give new parents a few weeks to adjust. Not my circle of friends and acquaintances. We had all our neighbors visit to see the new member of our culdesac. If I needed these visits to be short and sweet, my friend the commode would trickle to my rescue. It's amazing how quickly I could get rid of guests just by saying, "I'm sorry, but I need to go to the bathroom now," while pointing to my little friend. People would stumble all over themselves to get out the door. They probably laughed themselves home.

Bringing my little Riley home threw a huge wrench in my well tuned machine called life with a bump and two casts. I thought I had finally figured everything out, and had developed a workable routine. Now I had to change diapers.

My original diaper changing solution was absolutely ridiculous! Our changing table was located in the baby's room, so if I was all settled in the T.V. room, I would:

1. Put the baby in the infant car seat.

2. Stand up and balance myself on one leg.

3. Move the walker forward a few inches.

4. Hop forward.

5. Reach back and drag the car seat behind me.

6. Repeat steps 3 - 5 all the way down the hall until I reach the baby's room.

This was my routine every time the baby needed a diaper change. The most challenging part once I reached the changing table was getting the baby out of the car seat, which was on the floor, and up to the changing table without either dropping him, or toppling over myself. It didn't occur to me to put the car seat with the baby in it on the changing table to get him out. Perfect demonstration that functioning legs are required for a functioning brain.

How many times does a newborn's diaper need to be changed?

How quickly to do you usually need to respond to a newborn's discomfort and screaming?

I know, ridiculous!

After few days of this routine - apparently, depression also affects learning ability - I set up a changing station in the T.V.

room.   The similarities between this movable changing station and my commode were not lost on anyone.

The response from first time spectators to our current family sport were pretty typical.   They would start with the standard sympathetic, "Awwwwww . . .", and quickly turn into a smirk, and eventually a giggle when they saw the commode.   This entire response was repeated from the beginning when they saw me attempt to walk.   At the time, I was appreciative of the company and caring of the few brave souls who ventured from their own busy family lives to enter my solitary, hilarious, monotonous existence, so I didn't mind the reactions.   My welcomed visitors also helped me clear away the oppressive cyclone of emotions that I relate to being depressed.   If I could temporarily divert my energy into entertaining my guests, rather than entertaining myself with the numbness induced by watching paint dry (aka, daytime T.V.), I could also temporarily divert the winds of my depression cyclone. Things like depression cannot exist without secrecy and solitude. I am sure that the same can be said of other life altering, destructive behaviors such as addiction, abuse and oppression. If you ever find yourself giving in to the emotions that lead you to choose one of these behaviors, or are living with someone else who does, call someone, knock on someone's door, GET OUT!

If, like me, the person with whom you share your deepest confidence is right there in the thick of it too, talk to as many of your friends and family members as you can. This will help show the true character of those around you. The ones who look at you with that shocked, "OMG, I've got to get out of here!" look are to be immediately removed from your Christmas card list. Simply show the door to those few relatives whose solution it is to move in, take control of your life and 'make it all better'. These are probably the same people who encourage or display those destructive behaviors I just mentioned. The rest, as long as they don't call the local mental hospital unless absolutely necessary, can be counted as true friends. Hopefully, someone will shine through and help. I truly believe that when you are ready and willing, help is always available. As I tell my now 9 year old Riley, "We can't help you unless you use your words. Fortunately, I don't have ears that can hear your thoughts."

Luckily, I had a few good friends that came by occasionally, brought meals and took Evan for play dates. I didn't have any close family members except those to whom I would gladly show the door, and my mother-in-law was busy healing herself with my father-in-law stumbling through their household chores, so Duane and I hopped along this journey alone together. Another situation that would probably have been faced by Romeo and Juliet, I'm guessing.

Visitors were always shocked to see our sparkling clean house, Evan's neatly laundered clothes and our fully stocked pantry and 'frig. Duane walked this, "Road less travelled" with the same manic dedication to the tasks at hand that he did when I went into early labor with Evan, only there wasn't any bark to be shoveled. Instead, he tackled the grocery shopping, laundry, dusting, vacuuming and commode duty as if his life depended on the successful conclusion of each task. Every time friends came to help, the only chore available was sitting and talking with me.

Gee, Darn!

I'LL TAKE DOOR NUMBER 362, PLEASE!

The everyday tasks like diaper changing and dishes were becoming easier the longer I patiently hopped through them. I had my most anticipated doctor appointment to remove my right cast when Riley was three weeks old. Those three weeks brought a relief from OB and Orthopedic appointments, and a corresponding relief from co-pays..

Duane commented on my chipper mood as we arrived in the hospital parking lot, and he disappeared to find a wheel chair. A few minutes later, safely ensconced in the chair with Riley snuggled in his infant car seat cradled in my lap, and Evan hitching a ride on my knees, we arrived at the back of the line for the Orthopedic check-in. Duane parked my chair next to the children's play area a little way away from the line so Evan could stay amused during the wait. I oooh'd and m'hmmm'd distractedly at Evan's demonstrations, thinking about the bath I would take when we got home, and wondering if we had enough of Evan's bubble bath left.

I kept track of my husband's progress through the line, and started getting a little knot of excitement in my stomach when he finally stepped up to the window. He was at the window longer than normal I thought, but finally he started walking toward us, looking a little nervous.

"Well, there was a problem," he said quietly, "but I fixed it." he added quickly.

"What do you mean, 'problem'?" I asked jumping immediately to '10' from my '3' on the anxious scale, and going the opposite direction on my happy-meter.

"Apparently," he started slowly, "they didn't only cancel the remainder of your OB appointments after Riley was born, they cancelled ALL your appointments. You weren't even down on their books today to have your cast removed."

"WHAT?!" I said in stupefied surprise.

"But, . . . but . . . " I spluttered.

"I know, I know," he placated, his hands making gestures as if trying to physically push my anxiety down a few notches.

"I told the guy at the check-in window that you wouldn't leave until that cast came off, even if you had to rip it off yourself, and that If he wanted a peaceful lobby he would find a way to fit you in."

"You got that right!" I said as threateningly as possible while sitting in a wheel chair with an infant car seat on my lap and my pink and blue sticks propped up on those foot rests.

My original appointment was at 10:30 a.m. and one of the technicians kindly fit me in after the last appointment and during his lunch at 12:30. That was certainly not in his job description in this age of HMO's, PPO's and SOB's, so I kept spluttering my gratitude and thanks until I was distracted by my ape-like leg emerging from the plaster. I had honestly not thought of the consequences of not shaving for seven weeks. I remember being amused by the thought that I could move back to U.C. Berkeley and fit right in now. Naturally, I wore shorts to the appointment given my oven-like body temperature because an infant was constantly attached to my milk jugs, so I was quite embarrassed and glad the place was deserted for lunch. The technician had obviously heard and seen all this before, and proceeded to fit me with a walking boot, which was thankfully removable for the bath I had planned.

With the ability to finally see and scratch my leg (what a glorious feeling!), I started to feel a small sense of normalcy, and the winds of my emotional cyclone calmed even further. I could see a hint of blue skies through my cloud-filled life, but not enough to make a Dutch boy's pants.

What? You've never heard to look for enough blue in a cloudy sky to make a Dutch boy's pants?

Ask Jean, my Mother-in-Law. That is one of her North Dakota sayings. Since I've never been to Holland, I don't know how a Dutch boy's pants differ from an American boy's pants. Oh, well . . . just another day at the melting-pot zoo.

The walking boot on my right leg didn't make much difference in my life, except during sleeping and bathing. I found out that I still couldn't take a bath, because when I stood up to dry off, all the water drained off my body into my remaining cast before I could soak it up with a towel.

See **The Birth** chapter for details on the consequences.

I could, however, take my daily sponge bath and at least wash, dry and shave one leg. Ladies, if you ever want to know what your legs would look like if you were a man, although I don't know why you would, have a cast put on your leg and leave it there for seven weeks. Not only was my body not my own because I just had a baby check out of my one-of-a-kind 5-Star Baby Hotel, complete with umbilical cord room service AND maid service, but now I also had one stick-skinny, hairy man-leg and one blue cast.

I headed strait for the bathtub when I got home, even if I couldn't actually take a bath. Sitting on the edge with one cast out and one hairy leg in, it took three razors before the job was finished and I was somewhat satisfied with the result. Sickly pale and stick straight, I felt entirely confident that this was the only time any part of my body would ever resemble that of a Runway Model.

One free leg also brought a slight relief while sleeping. I now had to prop only one leg up on a pillow. Try to sleep every night for almost three months with both feet higher than your heart, while providing a soft, comfy bed for an 8 month old fetus that rests on all your abdominal organs and your spine, I dare you! I was now much more comfortable with one leg, and a newborn positioned anywhere I wanted. Thankfully, this gave me one third fewer obstacles to a good night sleep - I still had to find a comfortable position twice a night for a nursing newborn and a cast clad left leg.

Now that I no longer had a baby tap dancing on my bladder, I no longer needed my potty chair. Once my first cast was removed, I said good bye to this wonderful device.

I feel sure, however that I will see it again, someday. I'm sure Duane hopes that the LVN at the home will have taken over his job by then.

Four weeks after the removal of the first cast, the second came off. It was a little anti-climactic in that no balloons or confetti dropped from the ceiling of the hospital room, no trumpet call sounded from somewhere off camera and no middle-aged man came out of a door holding a microphone and a large cardboard check with lots of zeros, but I couldn't have felt more excited if that particular dream had come true. I can honestly say, that day was one of the happiest of my life, and I still tearfully remember this as the first time I walked on my own, with the help of my left walking boot, while cuddling my little Riley in my arms. My independent streak was finally able to resurface, and it has been safely ensconced in my life ever since - albeit with a few more healthy modifications. I continue to forcefully subdue the impatience character trait, however, which has been extremely helpful in raising my boys to the age where they are trying to break down the door to puberty. We'll see how my resolve holds as we rocket our way to manhood. **Learning when to subdue my impatience, and when to let it fly** has actually helped the most in smoothing my successful entrepreneurial path - Life Lesson #3, thank you!

I think that during this time in our marriage I was quite overdrawn in my spousal bank account. Luckily, I had deposited quite a bit in between my incidents so he knew I was a good risk. Duane is a Tax Man by the way, an Enrolled Agent to be precise, so I know of what I speak. Combine that with his artistic abilities, and I have a one-of-a-kind to be sure. Our landscaping and our finances are truly unique.

Once my self-pity depression cyclone started to abate, I opened my eyes to three more life altering, earth shattering realizations:

I ceased viewing my husband as simply the man with whom I share parenting duties, meals and incredible night time activities when non cast-laden (again, you have no idea how much functioning legs are required for a functioning libido). I know now that my husband is truly my partner in life, and there is no one better suited to that task and title. As Brandi Carlile puts it in her song, "All of these lines across my face, tell you the story of who I am." I have been unbelievably fortunate to have my man present at the creation of each and every line and gray hair, and this experience created quite a few. I just hope I live up to his expectations half as well . . . and that my curvy figure stays at least in the same neighborhood.

Remember that "Walk 'till you know where you're going" quote from earlier? Well, now I know where I'm going. That "Road less traveled" is getting lots of wear, because I have now made some definite choices about my life and the lessons I want my sons to learn.

I will also never again say that I can't do something. I won't even think it! I'm not talking about just a "glass half full" kind of attitude, because I have pretty much been that way all my life - to my husband's occasional irritation. (I think twice now before making instinctual pollyanna comments, however.) No, I have actually learned that if I can go through labor and delivery, care for a three year old, a newborn, a home and a husband with the limitations imposed by the fact that I'm hopping through life as a pink and blue flamingo, **I CAN DO ANYTHING!** I have since proven this to be true through my business and this book you are reading, because ~

Wonder Woman has nothin' on me!

I have an hourglass figure too!

Okay, my figure is less hourglass and more sandbags.

I have cool transportation too!

Okay, my walker isn't invisible, and moves a little slower than a plane.

I have a Super Hero husband who cleans toilets!

HA!

THE BUSINESS
CAN'T SEE THE FORREST FOR THE GUMP

If you are too young to have seen the movie Forrest Gump, go download it on your iPad, Wii, PS3, X-Box or Internet ready TV, and learn a little about life and chocolate. The whole theme of the movie is summed up in one sentence spoken by Forrest himself in the last 15 minutes of the movie, and describes perfectly my philosophy about my own life.

My life, and maybe yours, is a combination of random chance and destiny. There is very little I can do to affect either . . . or is there?

If I choose to drive 90 mph down the freeway, weaving in and out of traffic, I am increasing the odds that death is my destiny. Likewise, what are the chances of my taking too large a step out a neighbor's front door when I can't see my feet and have poor balance, and landing with two broken legs? All of the situations I have outlined in this book happened because of a series of events, during which a change in any one decision could have altered the path of destruction. As Albus Dumbledore says, "It is our choices that show what we truly are, far more than our abilities." ~ J.K. Rowling. The same holds true in business. And, each new choice has the potential to broaden your mind to a new experience. Once broadened, your mind cannot diminish back to its previous blissfully ignorant state. You are then ready and open to broaden even further, and you start to grow exponentially. This is what separates the adventurous and, to me, the successful from the simply satisfied.

In this way, I believe that our own choices determine our destiny.

Every time I turn on the television or listen to the 20 something mom's gossip while I'm waiting to pick up my nine year old, I have confirmation that my choices have kept me in this Robert Frost poetic version of life. Not only do these unique choices apply to my personal life, but they have helped me create a very unique professional life.

As I mentioned, I went back to Blue Ribbon Personnel after the holidays of 2001, and settled back into my professional staffing role, more commonly and not so fondly referred to as 'Head Hunting'. I quickly discovered, however that I had completely lost that hunger and drive to sell people. If I was going to sell, I now wanted to sell something that could not decide to up and move across the country two months after telling me that San Francisco is the perfect city in which to live, and the job I just presented them is the perfect job. Really, head hunting is actually selling people. I would find someone with specific skills and experience, sell them to a company looking for those skills, collect a good fee and then hope like hell the new employee could actually do what they and their previous employers and references said they could do.

Yes, I did check references.

I didn't just wake up one day and decide I was no longer an employment trafficker. I was actually overtaken by a new, blinding obsession, that is other than my obsession with my children.

During my pregnancy with Evan in the summer of 1998, I was so overjoyed and shocked that we had finally gotten an embryo to stick that I felt as if I had passed one of the hardest tests in the journey of life - procreation. I went to my Windows 98 PC and tapped out a report card in Excel that looked like this:

Fall Semester Report Card

Class Title	Grade
Pregnancy 101	A+
Pregnancy Prevention 101	F

I had seen sports shops in the mall that put designs on shirts for people, and thought, "I wonder if they can put this on a maternity shirt?" Target had plain white cotton maternity shirts for $10, so I bought a couple and brought them and my report card printout to the mall.

The bored kid behind the counter said, "Sure we can do that, but it will take about half an hour."

I wore my new shirt out shopping for baby stuff the next weekend, and got stopped so many times by people commenting that I didn't get any shopping done. Every time I wore the Report Card shirt, I experienced a repeat of the first.

I remember thinking, "I could pull out duplicates of this shirt from my purse and sell them to passersby."

Before these thoughts could materialize into anything more concrete, however, I started feeling cramps and was hospitalized for early labor.

For the next three years I was quite preoccupied by my precious little son and several job changes until I was finally able to pull out my maternity wardrobe again when I started showing for my next pregnancy.

Early in this pregnancy at about four months, I had to take a business trip to Kansas City, MO. I had already started wearing some of my maternity clothes because I was at that "Is she or Isn't she?" stage.

I wore my Report Card shirt on the plane, and a woman stopped by my seat after we boarded and said, "I'm so glad you are on this flight! My husband and I saw you in the airport and I wanted to ask where you got that shirt, because my daughter is a teacher and she is pregnant. It would be the perfect gift for her."

Blinding, bright spot light shining in my eyes with a dawning obsession!

I told the woman that I had it made for me in a local sports shop, and that she could do the same. She said that that was too bad and that she was hoping there was somewhere she could go to buy it.

The light as well as the obsession got so bright that I couldn't

sit still!

I pulled out my purse, searched for my planner, and started

feverishly jotting down ideas for more shirts.   Here are a few

results from that four hour in flight solo brainstorming session:

Made from

Mommy and Daddy's

RECYCLED MATERIALS

Operating System
Loading

Please wait 9 months

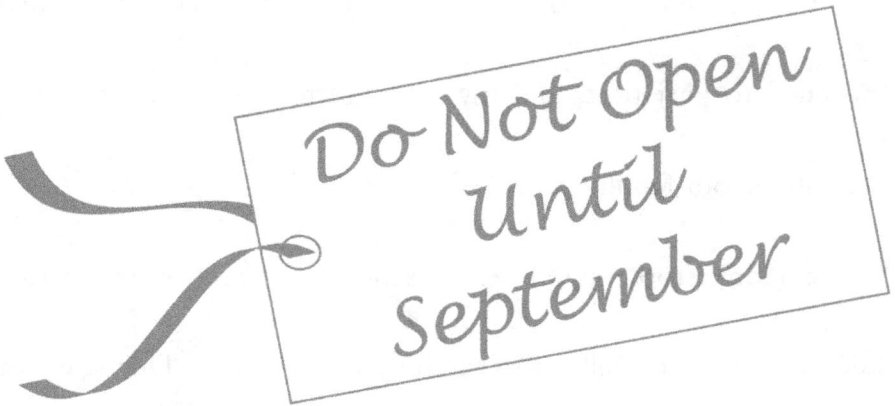

Do Not Open Until September

That night when I called my husband and son to say good

night, I mentioned the woman in the airport, but didn't say

anything about my new designs or the obsession that had taken hold of me so strongly that I was a little frightened.

Then I lost my job.

Then I got a new job.

Then I broke my legs.

Then I had a baby.

My lack of drive and subsequent decrease in income when I returned to Blue Ribbon were masked by the fact that I had switched to part time, and my husband took over the financial security of our family.

I couldn't stop thinking of this new idea, and by the fall of 2002 couldn't stop talking to my husband about it. Duane is not a big financial risk taker, so it took a long time and a lot of solid research on my part before he started warming up to the idea. The internet was almost as old as Evan, and I couldn't find a single novelty maternity company, let alone product that came up in my Google searches.

My obsession grew stronger.

If no one was there yet, I could be the first, and have a competitive edge. My husband's interest warmed further.

"But I don't know anything about starting a business," I told myself.

"How would I do it?"

"Where would I run it?"

"Where would I get the money to start it?"

"What about Blue Ribbon?"

"My kids are too young - they need me!"

The prospect of starting a novelty maternity company produced the same kind of shock and disbelief as the confirmation by the E.R. Doctor that I had broken both my legs.

Only, the tornado swirling around me now was fear mixed with excitement rather than depression.

If I could handle that original cyclone, and get through that situation of broken legs while pregnant, I told myself, I know I can do something as simple as start a business.

The lies we tell ourselves when we are naive first timers allow for many people's brains to expand and form them into budding entrepreneurs..

My profession at the time gave me an incredible advantage. If I wanted to start an internet business, internet techies were readily available. I started calling some of my most trusted placements, and asking their advice. My brain and confidence expanded further.

I learned about the creation of a website and credit card processing. I came up with a name based on the book I read to my boys every night - 'Mama Loves'. I thought that people would be confused about which spelling of 'Mama' to use, so I changed

it to 'Mommy Loves', and my obsession became a business - a

home based business.

The next question I needed answered was, "Where am I going

to get some money?"

Once my In-Laws heard what I was contemplating, and saw

what I had created thus far, they offered me $5,000 to start the

business. My Father-in-law was very fatherly in his advice, and

my Mother-in-law again praised me for my creativity.

Ever since I met Jean in 1979, she has praised me for my

creativity by way of belittling herself for her supposed lack of it.

I have played the Cello since junior high school, and my In-Laws

bought me a Cello a year after meeting me. Anytime I played

music, cooked a delicious meal, created a greeting card for a

friend or did some other fun, creative thing, Jean would respond

in the same way:

"Wow! I wish I was as creative as you are! I must have been standing in the wrong line for the wrong door when they were handing out creativity, because I didn't get any of this when I was born. You have more creativity in your little finger than I have in my whole body!"

Almost 30 years later now, I can confidently say that she was wrong. Playing music, cooking and having fun with a computer are all nothing compared to creating and nurturing a responsible, loving human being. Anyone can force themselves out of their comfort zone to try something new and different, and I dare you to do just that! Jean created this amazing man for me to marry, and I just hope I can do the same for my future Daughters-in-law.

In March, 2003 I applied for a business license, advertised for a fictitious business name and secured the domain name, MommyLoves.com. That day was one of the most exciting and humbling I have ever experienced beyond childbirth. The mixture of arrogance and insecurity that was required when I used to fool myself into believing I was in control at all times was lifted by my 'broken legs while pregnant' experience. It was replaced with peace, confidence and a healthy dose of fear, and my mind was now open to the amazing possibilities. Since then, I have been flying between 1 and 10,000 feet in my own plane of business called MommyLoves. Sometimes I have to slow down long enough to see the forest of beautiful bumps for the shirts.

My husband's support meant everything. I couldn't raise our kids without his help and I certainly couldn't run a home based business without it. The day I secured the business license and the domain name bore the lightest steps along this road to self employment. The next eight months were filled with very few days of sunshine and smooth travel, even though I navigated the beautiful Northern California summer and early fall. Most of the time I felt as if I walked through muck and mire wearing full combat gear. Actually, this turned out to be the best test and training for my new career. The virtual bricks and mortar that set the foundation for MommyLoves were formed by the following:

1. Finding a manufacturer for my shirts that did not require a minimum order of 20,000 pieces of each size. This took at least five months of daily searches, emails and phone calls.

2. Finding a credit card processor that would not charge me additional fees I would then have to pass on to my customers.

3. Finding a good silk screener who could also produce high quality products in small quantities.

4. Designing and building the entire website, including the shopping cart, by myself with no previous internet or programming experience but a lot of help from some amazingly giving, geeky angels.

5. Securing a business address that was not a P.O. Box or my home address.

6. Finding a good marketing person who could produce a blossoming brand with my little seed money.

All this was accomplished while I was still working as a Head Hunter and taking care of my home and children. Riley was 18 months old, and had stopped taking naps three months prior. Evan was almost five. By November 1st, 2003 I was ready for launch. All that work had taken me 8 months - almost as long as another baby. I was now ready for the real work - filling orders.

I kept envisioning that old IBM commercial where a small band of workers at a startup were huddled around one computer as one of them pushes the key to publish their new website, and they all watch as the visitor tally rises exponentially. I was scared to death, and prayed to God that wouldn't happen to me.

It didn't.

There are countless books, video tapes and courses telling budding entrepreneurs how to become millionaires by following some formula.

This is certainly not one of them.

The path outlined in this book is worn by many successful choices, not dollars.

I was familiar with setting realistic and stretch goals, and had really only one strong desire for the reward of this business: To provide a reasonable income to replace my day job and enable me to stay home to raise my boys. I would plan for the "millionaire status" when my sons were raised and out of the house, because I have realized throughout my life's journey thus far that we can all have only one master. It takes time, energy and mastery to become a millionaire. It also takes time, energy and mastery to raise caring, productive young men who can hopefully make a difference in the lives of those around them. Fooling myself into believing that I could build a millionaire business and raise my sons the way I want would actually fulfill my mother's definition of "having my cake and eating it too!"

I had to choose, and I knew which path was most important to me. I chose to stand in the very short line, as my Mother-in-law would put it, for the door that opens for people who make their children and family their priority, while also continuing to broaden their own experiences. I specifically built my business to fulfill my one goal - independence that would allow me to become a Work At Home Mom (aka WAHM). January 1, 2005 saw the achievement of that goal.

NEVER, NEVER, NEVER GIVE UP
BREATHING WATER?

Since that date in 2005, I have had to consciously decide to never

give up, or give in! 65% of the WAHM's I have met online and in

person are working from home only until they can earn enough

money to hire a full time babysitter, nanny or "decent" day care.

In other words, their business (and consequently their ego) is

more important than the actual staying at home with the kids..

It was hard enough defending my decision to work 4 days a week in a corporate environment in 1998, then more difficult to work part time in the cut-throat world of Head Hunting Techies in 2000, I thought I wouldn't have to justify actually wanting to stay home with my kids when I joined the WAHM community. Not so. I found out that I was still traveling this grassy path that wanted wear, and would be doing so for the rest of my life, no matter what I do next, and those not on the path with me would always look at me as if I had gills and green scaly skin.

Surprisingly, fulfilling this WAHM goal opened my eyes further to realize another goal I didn't even know I had. I discovered countless other people and their businesses I could support to do the same. Yes, we are the minority, but there are billions of people, honey, so there are lots of us! This provided a wonderful twist to my traditional business model. I decided not to hire employees, but to contract work from vendors and support small businesses like mine.

I have had countless experiences confirming that I made the right decision, the most recent of which was not so pleasant. My wonderful Mother-in-Law died suddenly four months after a successful mastectomy and light chemotherapy treatments for her Breast Cancer. The cancer had already spread to her bones, unbeknownst to the Doctors, and mine was the last face she saw and the last voice she heard before passing away. 30 short years knowing and loving her taught me that time is really all we have, and how we spend that time is what determines the life we live and the true legacy we leave through the lives we touch. I really don't want to get to the end of my life and look into the faces of my loved ones with my eyes full of regret for all the things I didn't do or say. I don't want that to be the last thing they see of me. If I don't continue to invest in my children and family now, maybe no one will be there to look into my eyes as I die. I know that no fancy new car or larger, more lavishly furnished house is more important than spending time with my family, and showing them love and support.

I wish I didn't need the experience of breaking my legs while pregnant to teach me many lessons like:

• don't let fear hold me back from trying something new and believing in myself,

• nothing is as bad or as hard as it initially seems,

• be humble enough to slow down and enjoy life,

• don't let arrogance fool me into thinking I can control everything,

• say it now, don't wait for tomorrow unless I have no choice,

• do it now, too,

• when feeling down, do something kind for someone else - it will always make me feel better.

Ah well . . . thankfully I didn't break my neck. Hence, my favorite poem now beautifully framed in my family room, and my choice to continue on this less traveled road. So far, it has led me to incredible places full of amazing experiences.

Which fork in the road will I take next?

Whichever I choose!

You know the saying, "Whoever ends up with the most toys wins."?

Well I have changed that to:

"Whoever ends up with the most amazing, life altering experiences by personally and positively touching the lives of the most people wins."

Marrying an amazing man, graduating from college, riding horses daily on the beach, losing two potential bumps, growing two precious bumps, breaking bones, starting a business, losing a loved one and writing a book are sketches of my experiences thus far?

I hope you don't need a break in your life to get you to believe in yourself.

Where is your road leading you? Is it a sparsely populated, grassy road or are you following the backside of the other horses on the trail?

What adventures and dreams are you chasing?

Who are you nurturing along the way?

Who will be with you when you reach the end?

Which of the hopefully many amazing experiences will you reminisce with them about most?

What will they see in your eyes?

As you play out your life on this earthly stage . . . 'Break a

leg' (hopefully not two).

ABOUT THE AUTHOR

Mary Kathryn Johnson lives in the Northern California Sierra-Nevada Foothills with her husband, two sons and two Aussies.

Her days are filled with elementary school yard duty, writing, nurturing MommyLoves.com and wishing she could pursue all the dreams and inventions that seep into her mind. Hiking, skiing, reading and running with the pups (both human and canine) are her relaxation.

Mary wrote her first poem at age 8 entitled "This Tree Stands on the Hill", and fell in love with creativity and imagination. She learned to play the Cello at age 12, and equally enjoyed playing music by the Beatles and Bach (this love continues to the present day).

Visit www.MaryKathrynJohnson.com for more information about Mary, this book and the accompanying workbook.

If you have a story to tell visit www.HelpMeSelfPublish.com and tell it!